sixth&spring
books

Produced for Sixth&Spring Books by Penn Publishing Ltd.
www.penn.co.il
Editor: Shoshana Brickman
Technical editors: Rita Greenfeder, Tamara Bostwick
Design and layout: Michal & Dekel
Photographer: Roee Feinburg
Stylist: Roni Chen
Makeup artist: Perry Halfon

ISBN-13: 978-1-936096-07-7
Library of Congress Control Number: 2010921211

Manufactured in China
1 3 5 7 9 10 8 6 4 2
First Edition

CREATIVE CROCHET JEWELRY

By Esther Zadok

CONTENTS

Sunburst Ring, pages 116–118,
Mixed Metals Medley Ring, pages 125–127.

Golden Daisy Bracelet, pages 27–29, Gold and Silver Stretch Bracelet, pages 24–26,
Pearls on Ice Bracelet, pages 43–45.

Five Fingers Necklace, pages 77–79.

CHOREOGRAPHING CROCHET JEWELRY

For me, the art of crochet jewelry is a form of personal expression. It brings peace to the soul and is therapeutic in its essence. My path through dance and therapy flowed naturally to crochet jewelry. For as long as I can remember, I have danced and crocheted. Creativity is a mystery. It lies hidden inside each of us, yet defies our understanding. My parents raised me to give meaning to life, and to celebrate it. Dance has aided me and influenced my journey as an artist. Dancing with the crochet hook is my choreography.

Although I work from intuition and passion, creativity needs a solid technical base, too. Crochet stitches are the technique; the choreography is the jewelry. All the stitches in the world have been made; all the words have been spoken; all the steps have been danced. Creativity is what you make of these elements in the present.

My crochet jewelry is here for inspiration. Receive it as a personal gift, and dance with each piece as you make it, as the path of creativity leads you.

The projects in this book incorporate metallic thread, gold-filled wire, sparkling beads, elegant trimming and more. Each project is made using a single crochet hook, basic crochet stitches and lots of imagination.

With more than 30 projects, there is something to suit every taste and skill level. There are elaborate necklaces, sparkling rings, delicate bracelets and fun earrings. There are simple rings for beginners, and intricate bracelets for the more experienced crocheter. Some of the projects can be made in just a few hours; others present a rewarding challenge.

If you love to crochet but have never made crochet jewelry, now is the time to start. Alternately, if you love making jewelry but have never tried to crochet it, this book will teach you how. There are projects perfect for everyday wear, and others that merit very special events. While all of the projects are fabulous on their own, many can be part of a set.

Each project can be made exactly as described, or customized with your choice of thread, wire and beads. If you really love a design the first time you make it, try making it a second time with another type of bead or thread for a completely different result. For inspiration, look to nature, the colors you love, the emotions you are feeling, the people you meet, or the seasons of the year.

ESSENTIALS

Crochet abbreviations and terms

approx	approximately	**hdc**	half double crochet	**sl st**	slip stitch
bch	beaded chain stitch	**m**	meter	**st(s)**	stitch(es)
bdc	beaded double crochet	**mm**	millimeter	**tog**	together
beg	beginning	**prev**	previous	**tr**	triple crochet
bhdc	beaded half double crochet	**rem**	remaining	**tr-cl**	triple crochet cluster
bsc	beaded single crochet stitch	**rep**	repeat	**WS**	wrong side
ch	chain stitch	**rnd**	round	**yo**	yarn over
cm	centimeter	**roll st**	roll stitch	**yd**	yard
cont	continue	**RS**	right side	*(**)	repeat instructions following the
dc-cl	double crochet cluster	**sc**	single crochet	* (**)	as many times as written

Skill levels

◎ ◎ ◎ ◎ Beginner	These projects are for first-time crocheters and use basic stitches.
◎ ◎ ◎ ◎ Easy	These projects using basic stitches, but take a bit more time and require a bit more experience.
◎ ◎ ◎ ◎ Intermediate	These projects use a variety of techniques.
◎ ◎ ◎ ◎ Experienced	These projects use a greater variety of stitches and techniques and more complex finishings.

MATERIALS

Beads

"Endless" is the best description for my fascination with beads. When I enter a bead store, it is almost impossible for me to leave before closing time, and leaving without an assortment of irresistible beads in hand is out of the question. There are countless variations in color, size, finish and shape; these infinite possibilities often provide inspiration for the jewelry I make.

When making crochet jewelry with thread, make sure the beads you choose aren't too heavy. Amber beads are a great option since they can be very lightweight and come in a multitude of colors and shapes. Seed beads are also excellent for their light weight and many variations. Fire-polished beads (with an AB or matte finish), bicones, drops and pearls are also excellent additions to crochet jewelry. All the projects in this book can be made with any type and color of beads you like. Don't be afraid to let your imagination and creativity—and the beads you love—lead you.

Cuff bracelet bases

These are used to provide a sturdy base for crocheted bracelets. Be sure the crocheted piece you make completely covers the surface of the base you choose.

Clasps

There is a huge variety of clasps available. I tend to select box, sliding, T clasps and heart clasps to finish my pieces. Be sure to use high quality clasps since you want them to last a very long time.

Clothespins

I often use these to hold together glued items, such as crocheted bracelets and their bases, until the glue sets. Clothespins won't work with crocheted items that have protruding crystals or beads, but they are perfect for holding together flat items.

Crochet hooks

All of these projects require steel crochet hooks. I generally use the same size hook for all of my projects, but individual tension may affect your choice. If you work tightly, you may get more accurate results with a larger hook. Remember that crocheting is like handwriting—very individualized. It varies with the thread you use, the size of the crochet hook, and your own skill. Your choice of hook is largely a matter of your own personal preference. Consider how it feels in your hand and whether it is comfortable to use when working with thread or wire.

Crystals

Sparkling crystals add a special touch to crochet jewelry. I choose Swarovski crystals for their unrivaled beauty, high quality and incredible selection. One of my favorite ways of integrating crystals into crochet jewelry is to insert them into crocheted bezels (pages 21–22).

Crimp ends

These can be affixed onto thread tails to hold the tails together and provide a loop for attaching clasps or ear wires. Apply a dot of glue to the thread ends; then use a pair of flat-nose pliers to close the crimp end tightly. I often affix a bead or two onto the front of the crimp end to conceal it.

Ear posts, ear backs and clip-on posts

Ear posts are the straight pieces of wire that fit into pierced ears. They are secured to the ear with ear backs. If you don't have pierced ears, use clip-on posts instead.

Ear wires

Ear wires are available in many different styles. I often use wires shaped like a shepherd's crook since they slide easily into pierced ears. They are also easily attached: the loop at the front of the ear wire just slips onto a crocheted piece or crimp end.

Elasticized thread

This can be crocheted to make jewelry that is flexible and expandable. It eliminates the need for clasps on bracelets and makes them easy to put on and remove.

Fabric flowers

Flowers add an organic look to crochet jewelry. They can be sewn or glued onto the finished piece.

Hoop earrings

These come in many sizes and styles. They can be used on their own or along with ear wires to make crocheted earrings.

Measuring tape

You'll need this to make your jewelry symmetrical or exactly the right size to cover a cuff bracelet base. I recommend choosing a measuring tape that indicates inches and centimeters on the same side.

Metal chains

Incorporating chains into crochet jewelry creates an endless variety of possibilities, depending on the size and shape of the links.

Metallic thread

This type of thread imitates real gold and silver wire. It is available in a wide range of metallic colors and widths and is also easier to work with than wire. In these projects I have used Shinatex metallic Japanese thread because it is of very high quality, does not tarnish, and looks like real gold or silver. There are a number of other companies that produce metallic thread, including Sulky and DMC.

Multipurpose glue

This can be used to affix flowers and other decorative touches to the crocheted work, and to glue crocheted pieces to metal bases. Select glue that is easy to work with, has industrial strength and dries clear.

Needles

A variety of needles are suitable for crochet jewelry. Tapestry needles have a blunt point and a relatively large eye. You can use them to mark the outline for crocheted bezels, sew items together, or weave in tails when a project is finished. Sewing needles may also be used for marking outlines or sewing items together. Beading needles are useful for stringing beads onto thread.

Pliers

These are used for working with metal findings. Flat-nose pliers are used to close crimp ends. Round-nose pliers are used for opening jump rings.

Ribbon

Once you are skilled at crocheting, you can work with a wide variety of materials, including ribbon. Use any width or color of ribbon you like for an endless array of possibilities.

Ring shanks

Like all findings, these come in a wide variety of styles. I find them wonderful, especially because they are adjustable in size. Don't forget to use strong multipurpose glue to attach the crocheted piece to the ring shank.

Scissors

Use a pair of sharp scissors to cut thread and trim ends. Don't use them to cut wire, since this can dull the scissors.

Small hammer

When working with some wire pieces, you'll want to have a small hammer on hand to tap the crocheted piece flat.

Trimming

There are so many types of trimming—and they can add so much glamour to crochet jewelry. When selecting trimming for crochet jewelry, make sure the holes are large enough for inserting a hook.

Wire

In many projects, I use gold-filled or silver wire to make beautiful jewelry that is intricate, delicate and beautiful. You may also want to try crocheting with colored plated wire. Crocheting with wire takes practice and skill, so be patient if you are just starting out. When selecting the wire for your project, go for something soft and flexible. If you intend to string on beads, make sure the wire is thin enough to fit through the holes in the beads.

Wire cutters

Use these, rather than scissors, to cut wire.

STITCHES

Chain stitch (ch)

Make a slipknot.
Insert the hook in the
slipknot.

Yarn over and draw through
the loop on the hook to
make a new loop and
complete the stitch.

Continue until you have a
chain to your desired length.

Beaded chain stitch (bch)

Make a slipknot.
Insert the hook in the
slipknot. Slide 1 bead up the
thread, close to the hook,
and yarn over after the bead.

Draw the thread through the
loop on the hook, leaving
the bead at the front of the
work, lying on the chain.

Continue until you have a
chain to your desired length.

Beaded chain stitch (bch) with 2 (3) beads

Make a slipknot. Insert the hook in the slipknot. Slide 2 (3) beads up the thread, close to the hook, and yarn over after the beads.

Draw the thread through the loop on the hook, leaving the beads at the front of the work lying on the chain.

Continue until you have a chain to your desired length.

Single crochet (sc)

Working into the foundation chain.

Insert the hook from front to back, wrap the thread over hook, and draw the thread through the chain towards you, leaving 2 loops on the hook.

Wrap the thread over the hook again and draw through both loops on the hook, leaving 1 loop on the hook.

Beaded single crochet stitch (bsc)

Slide 1 (2, 3) beads up the thread, close to the hook. Insert the hook into the next stitch and draw the thread through so that there are 2 loops on the hook.

Wrap the yarn over the hook again and draw it through to complete the stitch.

Make sure the beads are in the right position before drawing the thread. Sometimes you'll need to pull the thread gently so that the beads are placed tightly.

Roll stitch (roll st)

Leaving a 4"/10cm tail, chain 6; join with slip stitch into the first chain stitch to form a ring. Yarn over 12 times, insert the hook into the ring, and pull up a loop. Yarn over and pull through all 14 loops on hook.

Double crochet (dc)

Wrap the thread over the hook, then insert the hook into the indicated stitch.

Wrap the thread over the hook again and draw the thread through the chain towards you, leaving 3 loops on the hook.

Wrap the thread over the hook again and draw it through the first 2 loops, leaving 2 loops on the hook. Wrap the thread over the hook again and draw it through the last 2 loops, leaving 1 loop on the hook.

Triple crochet (tr)

Wrap the thread over the hook twice, then insert the hook, from front to back, into the indicated stitch. Wrap the thread over the hook again and draw the thread through the stitch towards you, leaving 4 loops on the hook.

Wrap the thread over the hook again and draw it through the first 2 loops, leaving 3 loops on the hook. Wrap the thread over the hook again and draw it through the first 2 loops on the hook.

Wrap the thread over the hook again and draw it through the last 2 loops, leaving 1 loop on the hook.

Half double crochet (hdc)

Wrap the thread over the hook, then insert the hook, from front to back, into the indicated stitch. Wrap the thread over the hook again, and draw the thread towards you, through the indicated stitch, leaving 3 loops on the hook.

To finish the stitch, wrap the thread over the hook again and draw through all 3 loops on the hook. Leave 1 loop on the hook.

Slip stitch (sl st)

Insert the hook into the stitch. Yarn over and pull through both loops on the hook.

Double crochet cluster (dc-cl)

*Yarn over, insert the hook in the indicated stitch, and draw up a loop. Yarn over and draw through 2 loops on the hook; rep from * once. Yarn over and draw through all 3 loops on the hook.

Triple crochet cluster (tr-cl)

*Yarn over twice, insert the hook in the indicated stitch, and draw up a loop. Yarn over and draw through 2 loops on the hook—twice. Rep from * once. Yarn over and draw through all 3 loops on the hook.

Yarn over (yo)

Wrap thread over crochet hook.

BASIC TECHNIQUES

Affixing a clasp

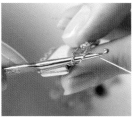

To affix the clasp, insert the tail into the appropriate clasp loop and make a slip stitch. Repeat at least twice so that the clasp is tightly secured. Cut the thread close to the work and apply a dot of glue.

Attaching crocheted pieces to ear wires or clasps

To complete many projects, you can use a tapestry needle (rather than a crochet hook) to weave tail ends into ear wires or clasps. If you choose this option, simply thread the tail of the thread through the needle's eye and weave as instructed.

Attaching multistrand clasps

Several necklaces and bracelets require multi-strand clasps. When securing several crocheted chains to a multistrand clasp, make sure you attach the same chain to the same loop on each side of the clasp. This ensures

that the piece hangs nicely. The method described below does not require any other tools or findings, and it is very secure when working with thread.

Gluing ends

I often apply glue to thread ends in order to secure them in place. I recommend using a wooden toothpick to transfer one drop at a time. (Too much glue can cause the chain to stiffen.) After the glue is applied, hold the glued parts together with your fingers for a few moments, until securely adhered.

Joining a crocheted chain into a ring with a slip stitch

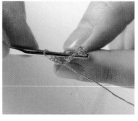

Some circular pieces require that you crochet in rounds. The basic stitches are the same, but you work around rather than in straight rows. To start, make a ring by joining a small chain with a slip stitch. Insert the hook, from front to back, through the first chain you made, wrap the thread over the hook, and draw it towards you through the chain and loop on the hook, as if working a slip stitch.

Making surface crochet

Insert the hook through the existing crocheted piece, and single crochet while using the finished piece as the foundation chain.

Passing thread from RS to WS

When finishing a piece, I often use the crochet hook to pass the thread from RS to WS. When I crochet a straight piece, for example, to make a bangle that will be glued onto a bangle base, I also use the crochet hook for ending.

With the aid of the hook, draw the thread tail to the WS of the piece. Make a slip stitch, then pull the thread carefully and cut the end close to the work.

Stringing beads onto thread

Stringing beads onto thread can be a bit tricky, even if the beads have relatively large holes. If you like, use a beading needle for stringing. You can also stiffen the end of the thread with a drop of nail polish. After the polish dries, the tip of the thread will be as stiff as a needle tip. When stringing beads onto thread, push the beads carefully down the thread.

Working in rows

When working in rows, you may need to add a turning chain stitch. This is an extra stitch that brings the hook up to the correct height for the next stitch to be worked. The longer the stitch, the more turning chain stitches you'll need. For example, if you're working in single crochet, you'll need one turning chain; if you're working in half double crochet, you'll need two turning chains; if you're working in double crochet, you'll need three turning chains; and if you're working in triple crochet, you'll need four turning chains.

Working single crochet into center of ring

Insert the hook, from front to back, into the center of the ring (not into the chain). When you have worked around the full circle, finish with a slip stitch into the top of the first stitch. Continue working in rounds.

Wrapping beaded thread around a bobbin

Some projects require a large quantity of beads, which can add considerable weight to your thread. You don't want this weight pulling the thread as you work, so I suggest wrapping the beaded thread around a bobbin. To prepare a bobbin, simply cut a 4"/10cm square of stiff cardboard and wrap the beaded thread around the cardboard. This bobbin supports the beaded thread as you work and helps prevent the thread from becoming tangled and difficult to manage. You may want to use more than one bobbin in a project; simply cut and tie another and continue. Find your own way of working and remember that the best technique is the one that is most comfortable for you.

SPECIAL TECHNIQUES

Crocheting into a metal chain

Working crocheted stitches into a metal chain gives more body and weight to your work. It also provides endless variations. The following instructions are for single crochet into a metal chain. Beaded single crochet can also be worked into a chain.

Insert the hook from front to back, wrap the thread over the hook, and draw the thread through the metal chain towards you, leaving two loops on the hook. Wrap the thread over the hook again, and draw through both loops on the hook, leaving one loop on the hook. Continue working this way, as described in the pattern.

Crocheting into trimming

With so many kinds of trimming, there are endless crochet jewelry possibilities. Find trimming with holes large enough for a hook to fit through and use it as the foundation chain when working single crochet.

Insert the hook from WS to RS into trimming hole, thread over the hook, draw the thread through the trimming towards you so that there are two loops on the hook. Thread over the hook and draw through both loops on the hook.

Making crocheted bezels

This technique is used to build secure bezels for flat-backed crystals. Applying a drop of glue to the back of the crystal before tucking it into the bezel helps secure the crystal in place.

Position the crystal on the crocheted piece. Thread a needle but do not tie a knot in the thread. Sew large stitches all around the crystal, marking its border.

Remove the crystal from the crocheted piece. With the thread and the crochet hook, pick up single crochet stitches all around the marked shape. Single crochet all around for the number of rounds indicated, then pull the thread to enlarge the last stitch. Do not cut the thread. Carefully remove the sewing thread.

Apply glue to the WS of the crystal, then insert into the crocheted bezel. Adjust until it fits snugly.

TIPS

Go with your instincts

You can crochet with just about any material, as long as you like the way it feels in your hand, the way it flows over your hook and the finished results. I hope you'll use the projects in this book as models and inspiration for projects you create on your own. Feel free to replace any of the materials and to use colors, bead types and textures you love.

Bead quantities

In some projects, I've listed exact quantities of beads; in others, I've given approximate weight values (in grams). All of these numbers are estimates since the amount of beads you use depends on the size and number of your stitches.

A word about gauge

You'll notice that I don't specify the gauge for any project. That's because crocheting, as I mentioned, is like handwriting—very individualized. The gauge of your work depends on your crochet style. The most important consideration is the final dimensions of the project you wish to make. On that basis, add or decrease stitches accordingly.

Beaded stitches

In the Stitches chapter (pages 13–17), you'll find detailed instructions (with photos) for the beaded single crochet (bsc) and beaded chain stitch (bch). In fact, almost any crochet stitch can be worked with beads. Simply follow the instructions for that stitch and incorporate one or two beads into it. Once you get the hang of it, you'll find it easy to integrate beads into other stitches, such as beaded half double crochet (bhdc).

GOLD AND SILVER STRETCH BRACELET

This bracelet is crocheted with elasticized gold and silver thread, creating a luxurious harmony of metals. I integrated a variety of gold beads, but you may opt for silver beads as well. Another notable element of this bracelet is the use of elasticized thread, which makes it easy to put on and take off. Make sure you choose beads with holes that are wide enough for slipping onto the thread.

Experience Level	Intermediate
Finished Measurements	Circumference: 7"/18cm; Width: 2"/5cm
Materials & Tools	- Elasticized gold thread (1mm), approx 33yd/30m - Elasticized silver thread (1mm), approx 33yd/30m - 30 round gold beads, 8mm - 20 round gold beads, 6mm - 14 antique gold-plated rosebud beads, 6mm - Steel crochet hook, U.S. size 4 (2.00mm) - Scissors - Multipurpose glue

Instructions

Randomly string all beads onto gold thread.

Foundation row: With silver thread and leaving a 4"/10cm tail, ch 65; join with sl st into 1st ch to form a ring. Do not twist.

Rnd 1: Sc in each ch around; end with sl st. Pull to secure, then cut thread, leaving a 4"/10cm tail.

Rnd 2: Attach beaded gold thread with sl st, ch 4, skip 1 st, bhdc in next st, ch 1, skip 1 st, hdc in next st, *ch 1, skip 1 st, bhdc in next st, ch 1, skip 1 st, hdc in next st; rep from * to end of rnd; end with ch 1, sl st into 3rd of 1st ch 4, sc in next ch-1 space.

Rnds 3–5: Rep row 2 three times. Pull to secure, then cut thread, leaving a 4"/10cm tail.

Rnd 6: Attach silver thread with sl st, ch 1, then sc in each st; end with sl st into 1st ch.

Rnd 7: Sl st into each sc around.

Ch 80; then pull to secure. Cut thread, leaving a 4"/10cm tail.

Randomly weave crocheted silver chain, from WS to RS, in spaces of crocheted bracelet.

Finishing

With crochet hook, weave tails from RS to WS. Cut tails close to the work and affix to WS with a dot of glue. Set aside until glue dries.

GOLDEN DAISY BRACELET

This bracelet features a bouquet of gold and pearl flowers. It is a modern version of a classic theme and is perfect for making a delicate but definite statement. This bracelet can be worn on its own or with the Golden Daisy Necklace (pages 86–88) and Golden Daisy Earrings (pages 113–115).

Experience Level   Experienced

Finished Measurements   Circumference: 7"/18cm

Materials & Tools

- Gold metallic thread, approx 33yd/30m
- 7 glass-based round pearl beads, 6mm
- Gold-plated 2-strand box clasp
- Steel crochet hook, U.S. size 6 (1.8mm)
- Scissors
- Tapestry needle
- Multipurpose glue

Golden Daisy Bracelet (bottom) and Golden Daisy Necklace, pages 86–88 (top).

Instructions

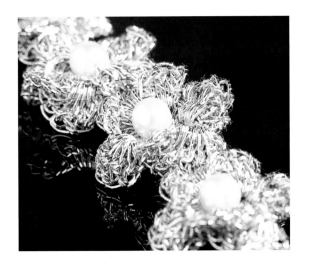

Rnd 4 [RS]: Ch 1, (1 sc, 1 hdc, 3 dc, 1 hdc, 1 sc) in each ch-5 space of rnd 3; join with sl st into 1st sc.

Pull to secure, then cut thread, leaving a 4"/10cm tail.

Draw both tails through hole in 1 pearl bead, from RS to WS, and a tie a secure knot. Cut tails close to the work and affix to WS with a dot of glue.

Finishing

With needle and gold thread, sew flowers tog in a row. Sew half of clasp onto first flower in row, and other half of clasp onto last flower. With crochet hook, weave all ends to WS and secure with dots of glue. Set aside until glue dries.

Flowers (make 7)

Leaving a 4"/10cm tail, ch 4; join with sl st in 1st ch to form a ring.

Rnd 1 [RS]: Ch 1, sc in center of ring, *ch 4, sc in ring; rep from * 3 times, ch 4; join with sl st into 1st sc.

Rnd 2: Ch 1, (1 sc, 1 hdc, 2 dc, 1 hdc, 1 sc) into each ch-4 space; join with sl st into 1st sc. Turn to WS.

Rnd 3 [WS]: Ch 1, 1 sc into 1st sc of rnd 1,*ch 5, 1 sc into next sc of 1st rnd; rep from * 4 more times, ch 5; join with sl st into 1st sc of this rnd. Turn to RS.

REGAL TRIMMING BANGLE

One of my childhood memories is of my mother's sewing cupboard, filled with an endless variety of gorgeous trimmings. We often sewed trimming onto clothing to make it a bit more special, or to give a new touch to something old. Still today, I love wandering through trimming shops and usually walk out with a few new varieties.

Experience Level	❁ ❁ ❁ ❁ Easy
Finished Measurements	Circumference: 7"/18cm; Width: About 2"/5cm
Special Techniques	Crocheting into trimming *(page 21)*
Materials & Tools	- Gold and black trimming, 1¼"/3cm wide, approx 8"/20cm - Gold metallic thread, approx 22yd/20m - Brass cuff bracelet base, 2"/5cm x 7"/18cm - Steel crochet hook, U.S. size 6 (1.8mm) - Scissors - Multipurpose glue - Clothespins (optional)

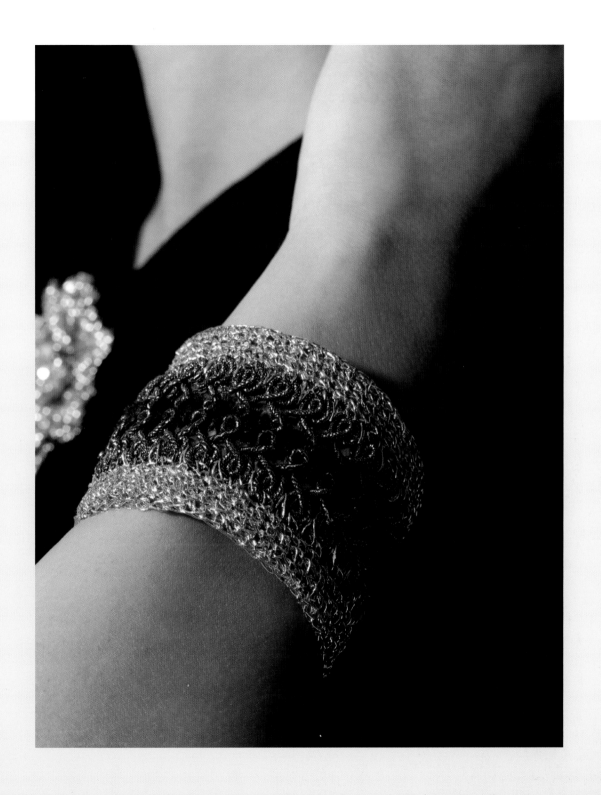

Instructions

Make a ½"/1.3cm fold at each end of the trimming. With thread, sc around entire trimming, working 2 sc in each corner. Cont around working sc in each sc and 2 sc in each corner until area of trimming and crocheted frame is large enough to cover bracelet base. Pull to secure, then cut thread, leaving a 4"/10cm tail.

Finishing

With crochet hook, weave tails to WS of work. Cut tails close to the work and affix to WS with a dot of glue. Set aside until glue dries. Lay crocheted piece on a flat surface, with WS facing up. Spread glue evenly on cuff exterior and WS of crocheted piece. Carefully place crocheted piece onto cuff, adjusting until it fits evenly. Hold pieces tog until firmly adhered (using clothespins, if you like), and set aside until glue dries.

CLASSIC GOLD BANGLE

This striking bracelet really shows off its delicate crocheted stitches, so be sure to practice crocheting with wire before making it. The classic design is perfect for wearing day or night, and it gives a touch of elegance to any outfit. Work slowly and enjoy the process when making this piece. The result is worth it!

Experience Level
 Experienced

Finished Measurements
Circumference: 7"/18cm; Width: About 2"/5cm

Materials & Tools

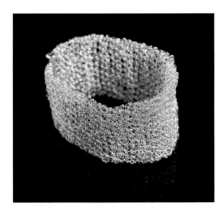

- Dead-soft gold-filled wire, 28 gauge (0.3mm), approx 33yd/30m
- Gold-plated 7-strand slide-lock clasp
- Steel crochet hook, U.S. size 6 (1.8mm)
- Wire cutters
- Small hammer

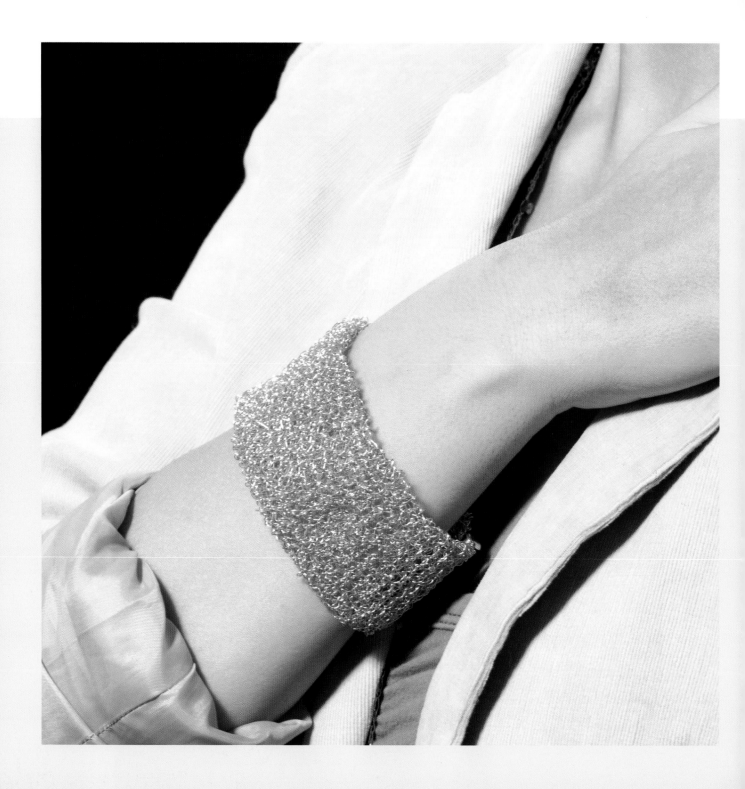

Instructions

Finishing

Lay crocheted piece on a flat surface and gently tap with a small hammer to flatten tube. With crochet hook, weave beg tail into loops on one half of clasp, weaving tail through each loop, then through crocheted piece, until clasp is securely attached. Cut tail close to the work and tuck in end. Rep as above with end tail and other half of clasp. Gently tap bracelet again with the hammer so that ends are neatly and tightly tucked into piece.

Leaving a 10"/25cm tail, ch 30; join with sl st into 1st ch to form a ring. Sc in each st all around until piece measures 7"/18cm, or to desired length according to wrist size. End last row with sl st into each sc. Pull to secure, then cut wire, leaving a 10"/25cm tail.

VIBRANT RAINBOW BANGLE

This versatile bracelet is crocheted with red wire and incorporates hundreds of tiny seed beads in a rainbow of colors. Though the beads are very small, stringing them on is actually quite easy since the wire is stiff. The bracelet can be worn flat or folded, creating wide-and-thin or narrow-and-thick options. The bracelet is reversible, too—the bold red wire is dominant on one side and the colored beads are dominant on the other. Although the instructions for this bracelet are simple, working with wire can be challenging because it tangles easily. I find it helpful to keep the wire in a small drawstring bag while I work.

Experience Level	◎ ◎ ◎ ◎ Intermediate
Finished Measurements	Circumference: 7"/18cm; Width: About 2½"/6.4cm
Materials & Tools	- Red color-coated copper wire, 28 gauge (0.3mm), approx 33yd/30m - Approx 400 red, orange, turquoise and yellow seed beads, size 11° - Steel crochet hook, U.S. size 8 (1.5mm) - Wire cutters

Instructions

NOTE:

The wire used in this project is flexible and can be stretched, so be careful not to make the bracelet too big.

Randomly string all beads onto wire. Leaving a 6"/15cm tail, work 50 bch, or as many bch sts necessary for desired length; join with sl st into 1st bch st to form a ring. Work bsc in every st all around. Cont working around in bsc until bracelet is 2½"/6.4cm wide, or desired width. End last round with sl st into each st. Pull to secure, then cut wire, leaving a 6"/15cm tail.

Finishing

With crochet hook, weave end tail a few times through bracelet. String though a seed bead, then weave again, leaving tail on WS. Cut tail close to the work, then tuck tightly into edge so end isn't felt or seen. Rep as above with beg tail.

EVENING AT THE OPERA BANGLE

The inspiration for this special bangle was my admiration for the way gold and silver jewelry accommodates gemstones in little bezels. I love crystals and believe they deserve a worthy bezel as well. Encasing glittering crystals with shiny silver thread is the perfect solution! After making this bracelet, you may want to try your hand at the matching Glamour Necklace (pages 68–72).

Experience Level	 Experienced
Finished Measurements	Circumference: 7"/18cm; Width: About 2½"/6.4cm
Special Techniques	Making crocheted bezels *(pages 21–22)*

Materials & Tools

- Silver metallic thread, approx 55yd/50m
- 1 Labrador square flat-back Swarovski crystal, 23 x 23mm
- 2 jet oval flat-back Swarovski crystals, 18 x 13mm
- 2 silver flare oval flat-back Swarovski crystals, 18 x 23mm
- Silver-plated cuff bracelet base, 2½"/6.4cm x 7"/17cm
- Steel crochet hook, U.S. size 6 (1.8mm)
- Multipurpose glue
- Black sewing thread
- Sewing needle

Evening at the Opera Bangle (bottom) and Glamour Necklace, pages 68–72 (top).

Instructions

Leaving a 4"/10cm tail, ch 6. Check gauge—16 ch should be 2½"/6.4cm long. If necessary, add or decrease number of chs.

Row 1: Sc in 2nd ch from hook and in each sc until end of row. Ch 1, turn—15 sc in all.

Rep row 1 until length is 7"/18cm.

Last row: Sl st into all sts to end of piece. Pull to secure, then cut thread, leaving a 4"/10cm tail.

NOTE: ────────────────

Be sure that each row has same number of sc until end.

Large square bezel

Fold crocheted piece in half, and *with black sewing thread and crochet hook, weave in a 1"/2.5cm piece of thread ½" from folded edge. The thread should be placed evenly between long edges of bracelet band. Rep from * on other side of fold.

Unfold crocheted piece and place on work surface. With silver thread, insert crochet hook into one marked side at midpoint of thread marker and surface crochet as follows:

Work 3 sc, turn work 90°, 6 sc, turn work 90°, 6 sc (after 3 sc you should be on opposite side and past black thread), turn work 90°, 6 sc, turn work 90°, 3 sc, sl st into 1st sc to make a square.

Work 1 sc in next 2 sts, 2 sc into next st, turn work 90°, *1 sc in next 5 sts, 2 sc into next st, turn work 90°, 1 rep from * 2 more times, 1 sc in next 3 sts. (You have now reached beg of square.)

NOTE: ────────────────────

Each corner of square has 2 sc in same st.

Pull thread to enlarge last st on hook; do not cut thread and remove hook. Carefully remove black thread. Spread glue evenly on the back of the square crystal and then carefully insert crystal into crocheted bezel, adjusting so that it is centered in the base. Set aside until glue dries. When glue is completely dry, insert crochet hook into the enlarged st, and pull thread to tighten loop to fit hook. Sl st around all sts of square. Pull to secure, then cut thread, leaving a 4"/10cm tail. With crochet hook, weave end tail to WS.

Small oval bezel (make 2)

Spread work on a flat surface. Place 1 oval crystal approx ½"/1.3cm to the right (left) of rightmost (leftmost) crocheted square bezel. Thread sewing needle with black thread, but do not tie a knot at the end. Leaving a 4"/10cm tail, make large sts all around oval crystal, marking its size. With silver thread and crochet hook, pick up sc around oval shape marked with black thread. Cont for 1 more round. Pull thread to enlarge last st but do not cut. Carefully remove black sewing thread. Spread glue evenly on the back of 1 oval crystal and insert crystal into bezel, adjusting so that it fits snugly into bezel. Rep with other oval crystal. Set bracelet aside until glue dries. Insert crochet hook into enlarged st on work and pull thread to fit hook. Sl st into all sts around crystal. Pull to secure, then cut thread, leaving a 4"/10cm tail.

Finishing

With crochet hook, weave tails to WS of work and cut tails close to the work.
Lay crocheted piece on a flat surface, WS facing. Spread glue evenly on cuff exterior and WS of crocheted piece. Place work carefully on cuff, stretching it a bit until it covers entire cuff. Adjust crystals, if necessary. Set aside until glue dries.

Clockwise from top left: Harvest Beads Bangle, pages 52–54, Evening at the Opera Bangle, Crocheted Flower Cuff, pages 55–57, Golden Daisy Bracelet, pages 27–29, Scrumptiously Scarlet Bracelet, pages 49–51.

PEARLS ON ICE BRACELET

This sparkling bracelet features jagged crystals and round pearls, along with pearly white seed beads. The soft gold thread sets off the beads beautifully, creating an elegant yet funky bracelet that can be worn day or night, for any occasion. Each chain in this bracelet is crocheted separately; then all seven chains are connected by a 7-strand slide lock. This lets the bracelet hang freely yet securely on the wrist.

Experience Level	Easy
Finished Measurements	Circumference: 7"/18cm to 8"/20cm

Materials & Tools

- Metallic gold thread, 30 gauge (0.2mm), approx 33yds/30m
- Approx 86 pearly white seed beads, size 6°
- Approx 20 glass-based round pearl beads, 6mm
- Approx 20 glass chip beads, 5mm
- Gold-plated 7-strand slide-lock clasp
- Steel crochet hook, U.S. size 6 (1.8mm)
- Scissors
- Multipurpose glue

Instructions

Finishing

Lay beaded chains on a flat surface. With crochet hook, weave beg tail of 1st chain through 1st loop of one half of clasp. Pull gently, then sl st into 1st ch of finished chain. Draw tail through same loop one more time and sl st into next 2 sts. Pull to secure, cut tail close to the work, and apply a tiny drop of glue to affix. Weave end tail of same chain through 1st loop of other half of clasp and rep from *. Rep as above with rem 6 chains, making sure you secure each chain to corresponding loops on clasp halves. Set aside until glue dries.

Beaded chains (make 7)

NOTE: ———————————————

Measure the 1st chain around your wrist to make sure it is the right size. Make the next 6 chains exactly the same length, so that the bracelet is balanced.

String a random assortment of 18 beads onto thread. Leaving a 4"/10cm tail, ch 3, sc into 1st ch from hook, 1 bch, turn, and sc into 2nd ch from hook, *1 bch, turn, 1 sc; rep from * until all beads are used, or until chain is 7"/18cm long or desired length. Pull to secure, then cut thread, leaving a 4"/10cm tail.

DAZZLING BLUE ZIRCON BANGLE

I made this eye-catching bangle for my daughter's graduation party. It takes a bit of time, but the results are stunning. Perfect for any evening occasion, it can be worn on its own or as a set with the Dazzling Blue Zircon Earrings (pages 95–97).

Experience Level	◎ ◎ ◎ ◎ Experienced
Finished Measurements	Circumference: 7"/18cm; Width: About 2½"/6.4cm
Materials & Tools	- Gold metallic thread, approx 33yds/30m - 400 blue zircon bicone Swarovski crystal beads, 4mm - Gold-plated cuff bracelet base, 2"/5cm x 7"/18cm - Steel crochet hook, U.S. size 6 (1.8mm) - Scissors - Multipurpose glue

Instructions

NOTE: ———————————————

For first 42 rows, WS is facing.

NOTE: ———————————————

Every row of crocheted beads ends with bsc with 3 beads. Every row with no beads ends with sc.

String all beads onto thread and wrap beaded thread around bobbin.

Leaving a 4"/10cm tail, ch 15, turn.

Row 1: Sc in 2nd ch from hook and in each ch across—14 sc. Turn.

Row 2: Ch 1, sc in each sc—14 sc. Turn.

Row 3: Ch 1, bsc in each sc—14 bsc. Turn.

Row 4: Ch 1, sc in each sc—14 sc. Turn.

Rows 5–40: Rep rows 3–4 another 18 times in all or until bracelet is 7"/18cm, or desired length.

Rows 41–42: Rep row 2 twice. Turn work, so that RS is facing.

Next Row (RS): Begin crocheting along long edge of bracelet as follows: ch 1, 1 sc in each of next 2 sts, *bsc with 3 beads in next sc, sc in next sc; rep from * until you reach the last 2 rows (without beads), work 1 sc in each of last 2 sc.

Next Row: Ch 1, turn work 90°, sc in each sc—14 sc.

Next Row: Ch 1, turn work 90°, 1 sc in each of next 2 sc, *bsc with 3 beads in next sc, sc in next sc; rep from * until you reach the last 2 rows (without beads), work 1 sc in each of next 2 sc.

Next Row: Ch 1, turn work 90°, sc in each of rem 14 sc.

Cont working around bracelet in this manner until piece is 2"/5cm wide (or wide enough to completely cover cuff); end row with 1 sc in next 2 sc.

Pull to secure, then cut thread, leaving a 4"/10cm tail.

Finishing

Draw tail through last loop, remove crochet hook, and tighten loop. With crochet hook, weave tail into WS of crocheted piece. Cut tail close to the work and affix to WS with a dot of glue. Lay crocheted piece on a flat surface, WS facing. Adjust beaded rows so that they are orderly and flat. Spread glue evenly on cuff exterior and WS of crocheted piece. Carefully position crocheted piece on cuff, then hold tog until pieces are firmly affixed. Set aside until glue dries.

SCRUMPTIOUSLY SCARLET BRACELET

This bracelet is crocheted with an assortment of red beads in a variety of textures and sizes. It is a perfect design for making use of leftover beads. For maximum effect, I wear the bracelet with a solid-colored dress. (A little black dress is just right!) The look is an expression of my personal belief that nothing in life is a single shade, and that even when things seem to be of uniform color, there is always a twinkling of variation.

Experience Level   Intermediate

Finished Measurements   Circumference: 7"/18cm; Width: About 2½"/6.4cm

Materials & Tools

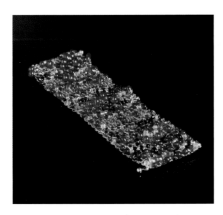

- Gold metallic thread, approx 55yd/50m
- Approx 150 fire-polished crystal beads, 4mm
- Approx 150 fire-polished red beads, 4mm
- Approx 250 seed beads, size 4°, 6°, 8°
- Steel crochet hook, U.S. size 6 (1.8mm)
- Gold-plated 11-strand slide-lock clasp
- Scissors
- Multipurpose glue

Instructions

Finishing

With crochet hook, weave beg tail into loops on one half of clasp several times, weaving tail through each loop, then through crocheted piece, until clasp is securely attached. Cut tail close to the work, and apply a dot of glue to secure.

Rep as above with end tail and other half of clasp.

Randomly string all beads onto thread and wrap beaded thread around bobbin.

Row 1: Leaving a 12"/30.5cm tail, ch 16.

Row 2: Sc in 2nd ch from hook and in each ch to end of row—15 sc. Ch 1, turn.

Row 3: Work 1 bsc in each sc—15 bsc. Ch 1, turn.

Rows 4–32: Rep rows 2 and 3 until work measures 7"/18cm, and ending with row 2, sc in every st—15 sc. Ch 1, turn.

Sl st into each st to end. Pull to secure, then cut thread, leaving a 12"/30.5cm tail.

HARVEST BEADS BANGLE

This beaded bangle features crochet stitches and lots of beads, but the beads are glued rather than crocheted on. The base is a brass cuff bracelet. The sides are edged with crocheted gold thread, and the colorful center is made by gluing on hundreds of colorful seed beads. I used leftover beads collected from old projects; if you have a color scheme in mind, select beads to match.

Experience Level	✿ ✿ ✿ ✿ Intermediate
Finished Measurements	Circumference: 7"/18cm; Width: About 2½"/6.4cm
Materials & Tools	- Gold metallic thread, approx 22yd/20m - Approx 100 grams seed beads, various sizes and colors - Steel crochet hook, U.S. size 6 (1.8mm) - Multipurpose glue - Brass cuff bracelet base, 2"/5cm x 7"/18cm - Clothespins (optional) - Scissors - Clear nail polish

Instructions

NOTE: ─────────────────────────

Make sure number of sts in chain is a multiple of 6 + 1 for pattern row.

Row 1: Leaving a 4"/10cm tail, ch 43 or until chain is 18"/46cm. Turn.

Row 2: Sc in 2nd ch from hook and in each ch to end of row, turn.

Row 3: Sl st into 1st sc, *skip next 2 sc, 5 dc in next sc, skip next 2 sc, sl st into next sc; rep from * to end. Pull to secure, then cut thread, leaving a 4"/10cm tail. With crochet hook, weave tails from RS to WS and cut close to the work.

Finishing

Lay crocheted piece on a flat surface, with WS facing. Spread glue evenly on cuff exterior and WS of crocheted piece. Carefully position crocheted piece on cuff, stretching if necessary, until piece frames the edges of the cuff. Hold tog until pieces are firmly affixed (using clothespins, if you like) and set aside until glue dries. Place beads in a shallow bowl or container. *Spread glue evenly on center of cuff and dip into bowl, rocking cuff back and forth until entire glued surface is covered with beads. Set aside until glue dries. Rep from * to make sure cuff surface is entirely covered with beads. Apply clear nail polish evenly over beads and set aside until polish dries.

CROCHETED FLOWER CUFF

This bangle is worked in two layers of crochet that are affixed on a brass gold-plated bangle. The first crocheted layer covers the bangle. The second layer consists of crocheted flowers, each of which features a sparkling crystal center. With this piece on your wrist, you'll feel as if you're wearing solid gold jewelry fit for a queen! The thrill, of course, is that you've made it with own hands using a simple crochet hook.

Experience Level　　 Experienced

Finished Measurements　　Circumference: 7"/18cm; Width: About 2½"/6.4cm

---

Special Stitches　　Roll Stitch: Leaving a 4"/10cm tail, ch 6; join with sl st into 1st ch to form a ring.
Yo 12 times, insert hook into ring and pull up a loop, yo and pull through all 14 loops on hook. *(page 15)*

Materials & Tools

- Gold metallic thread, approx 55yd/50m
- Brass cuff bracelet base, 1"/2.5cm x 7"/18cm
- 10 golden shadow flat-back round Swarovski crystals, 4mm
- Steel crochet hook, U.S. size 6 (1.8mm)
- Scissors
- Multipurpose glue
- Measuring tape
- Clothespins (optional)

Instructions

Row 1: Leaving a 4"/10cm tail, ch 8.

Row 2: Sc in 2nd ch from hook and in each ch to end of row—7 sc. Turn.

Row 3: Ch 1, sc in each sc—7 sc. Turn.

Rep row 3 until piece is 7"/18cm long, or large enough to cover cuff. Pull to secure, then cut thread, leaving a 4"/10cm tail.

Flowers (make 10)

Leaving a 4"/10cm tail, ch 6; join with sl st into 1st ch to form a ring. Ch 2, *roll st in ring, ch 1; rep from * 6 more times; join with sl st to top of 1st roll st—7 roll sts in all. Pull to secure, then cut thread, leaving a 4"/10cm tail. With crochet hook, weave ends from RS to WS and cut close to the work.

Finishing

Lay crocheted piece on a flat surface, with WS facing. Spread glue evenly on cuff exterior and WS of crocheted piece. Carefully position crocheted piece on cuff, adjusting so that piece covers entire cuff surface. Hold tog to secure (using clothespins, if you like) and set aside until glue dries.

Measure and mark 10 even intervals along cuff. Apply glue on WS of each flower, and at each interval, and attach to flowers. Apply glue to WS of each crystal and attach to center of each flower. Set aside to dry for 24 hours.

SHIMMERING CASCADE NECKLACE

This necklace features several large bead clusters, each of which is made up of dozens of small seed beads. The project requires quite a bit of concentration: you need to count the number of beads you use for each cluster to ensure that they are all the same size. The necklace can be worn long or wrapped twice around the neck.

Experience Level   ❁ ❁ ❁ ❁ Experienced

Finished Measurements   Length: 50"/127cm

Materials & Tools
- Gold metallic thread, approx 44yd/40m
- Approx 60 grams fire-polished Czech seed beads, olivine, honey, bronze colors, size 4°
- Steel crochet hook, U.S. size 6 (1.8mm)
- Scissors
- Multipurpose glue

Instructions

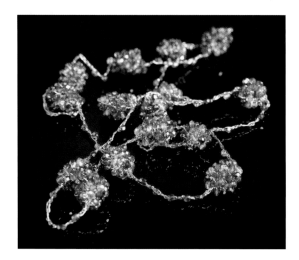

String all beads onto thread and wrap beaded thread around bobbin.

Leaving a 4"/10cm tail, ch 12; join with sl st into 1st ch st to form a ring.

**Next Rnd: Ch 15, including 4 random bch, ch 4, sl st into 1st ch of the ch 4 creating a loop.

Next Rnd: Work 2 bsc into each of the 4 chs of loop—8 bsc in all.

Next Rnd: Work 2 bsc into each bsc—16 bsc in all.

Next Rnd: *Skip 1 bsc, 1 bsc in next bsc; rep from * until you have decreased all sts.

Cont from ** 13 more times.

Next Rnd: Ch 15, including 4 random bch, ch 4; join with sl st into 1st ch of the ch 4 to form a ring.

Next Rnd: Work 2 bsc into each of the 4 chs of loop—8 bsc in all.

Next Rnd: Work 2 bsc into every 8 bsc—16 bsc in all.

Next Rnd: *Skip 1 bsc, 1 bsc in next bsc, rep from * until you have decreased all sts.

Finishing

Pull tightly to secure, then cut ends close to the work. Apply a drop of glue to each end to secure. To close necklace, slip beg loop over last crocheted bead.

REGAL EMERALD-STYLE NECKLACE

The seed beads that hang loosely from several thin crocheted chains give this necklace a sense of motion and elegance. It is perfect for wearing with a low V-neck collar and dresses up any outfit, day or night.

Experience Level	Intermediate
Finished Measurements	Length: 19"/48cm

Materials & Tools

- Gold metallic thread, approx 11yd/10m
- 290 transparent green seed beads, size 8°
- Gold-plated T clasp
- Steel crochet hook, U.S. size 6 (1.8mm)
- Scissors
- Multipurpose glue

Instructions

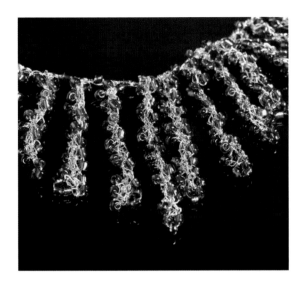

NOTE:

In this necklace, you'll make half the necklace chain, then 17 dangling chains (of increasing then decreasing length), then make the other half of the necklace chain.

String all beads onto thread.
Leaving a 4"/10cm tail, ch 3, *1 bch, ch 1; rep from * 17 more times—39 chs.
*Ch 1, 1 bch; rep from * 3 more times, ch 1, 1 bch with 3 beads.
*Ch 1, 1 bch; rep from * 3 more times, ch 1, sl st into 1st ch of prev row. Ch 1, 1 bch, ch 1.
*Ch 1, 1 bch; rep from * 4 more times, ch 1, 1 bch with 3 beads.
*Ch 1, 1 bch; rep from * 4 more times, ch 1, sl st into 1st ch of prev row. Ch 1, 1 bch, ch 1.
*Ch 1, 1 bch; rep from * 5 more times, ch 1, 1 bch with 3 beads.
*Ch 1, 1 bch; rep from * 5 more times, ch 1, sl st into 1st ch of prev row. Ch 1, 1 bch, ch 1.
*Ch 1, 1 bch; rep from * 6 more times, ch 1, sl st 1 with 3 beads.
*Ch 1, 1 bch; rep from * 6 more times, ch 1 sl st into 1st ch of prev row. Ch 1, 1 bch, ch 1.
*Ch 1, 1 bch; rep from * 7 more time, ch 1, 1 bch with 3 beads.
*Ch 1, 1 bch; rep from * 7 more times, ch 1, sl st into 1st ch of prev row. Ch 1, 1 bch, ch 1.
*Ch 1, 1 bch; rep from * 8 more times, ch 1, 1 bch with 3 beads.
*Ch 1, 1 bch; rep from * 8 more times, ch 1, sl st into 1st ch of prev row. Ch 1, 1 bch, ch 1.
*Ch 1, 1 bch; rep from * 9 more times, ch 1, 1 bch with 3 beads.
*Ch 1, 1 bch; rep from * 9 more times, ch 1, sl st into 1st ch of prev row. Ch 1, 1 bch, ch 1.
*Ch 1, 1 bch; rep from * 10 more times, ch 1, 1 bch with 3 beads.
*Ch 1, 1 bch; rep from * 10 more times, ch 1, sl st into 1st ch of prev row. Ch 1, 1 bch, ch 1.
*Ch 1, 1 bch; rep from * 11 more times, ch 1, 1 bch with 3 beads.
*Ch 1, 1 bch; rep from * 11 more times, ch 1, sl st into 1st ch of prev row. Ch 1, 1 bch, ch 1.
*Ch 1, 1 bch; rep from * 10 more times, ch 1, 1 bch with 3 beads.
*Ch 1, 1 bch; rep from * 10 more times, ch 1 sl

st into 1st ch of prev row. Ch 1, 1 bch, ch 1.

*Ch 1, 1 bch; rep from * 9 more times, ch 1, 1 bch with 3 beads.

*Ch 1, 1 bch; rep from * 9 more times, ch 1, sl st into 1st ch of prev row. Ch 1, 1 bch, ch 1.

*Ch 1, 1 bch; rep from * 8 more times, ch 1, 1 bch with 3 beads.

*Ch 1, 1 bch; rep from * 8 more times, ch 1, sl st into 1st ch of prev row. Ch 1, bch1, ch 1.

*Ch 1, 1 bch; rep from * 7 more times, ch 1, 1 bch with 3 beads.

*Ch 1, 1 bch; rep from * 7 more times, ch 1, sl st into 1st ch of prev row. Ch 1, 1 bch, ch 1.

*Ch 1, 1 bch; rep from * 6 more times, ch 1, 1 bch with 3 beads.

*Ch 1, 1 bch; rep from * 6 more times, ch 1, sl st into 1st ch of prev row. Ch 1, 1 bch, ch 1.

*Ch 1, 1 bch; rep from * 5 more times, ch 1, 1 bch with 3 beads.

*Ch 1, 1 bch; rep from * 5 more times, ch 1, sl st into 1st ch of prev row. Ch 1, 1 bch, ch 1.

*Ch 1, 1 bch; rep from * 4 more times, ch 1, 1 bch with 3 beads.

*Ch 1, 1 bch; rep from * 4 more times, ch 1, sl st into 1st ch of prev row. Ch 1, 1 bch, ch 1.

*Ch 1, 1 bch; rep from * 3 more times, ch 1, 1 bch with 3 beads.

*Ch 1, 1 bch; rep from * 3 more times, ch 1, sl st into 1st ch of prev row.

*Ch 1, 1 bch; rep from * 17 more times. Ch 3.

Finishing

Cut thread, leaving a 12"/30.5cm tail. Pull thread tightly to secure.

With crochet hook, weave end tail of crocheted chain into half of clasp. Pull tail through clasp twice, then weave into crocheted chain. Cut tail close to the work, then affix with a dot of glue. Set aside until glue dries.

Rep as above with beg tail and other half of clasp.

From left to right: Giant Flower Necklace and Pendant, pages 73–75, Cluster of Grapes Necklace, pages 65–67, Elemental Chain, pages 83–85.

CLUSTER OF GRAPES NECKLACE

When I was little, I often asked my mother about matching colors. "How do you know what goes with what?" I wondered. Her response was always the same: "Look at nature," she would say, "and the answer will be yours." As with many things in life, my mother was right. This necklace is dedicated to her, and to her ability to teach me that inspiration, like nature, is all around us. This necklace has a natural, organic feeling, as though one is wearing a tiny bouquet of flowers.

Experience Level	Intermediate

Finished Measurements	Length: 28"/71cm

Materials & Tools

- Gold metallic thread, approx 33yd/30m
- 20 olive crystal drops, 10mm
- 30 orange/white beads, 8mm
- 20 orange seed beads, size 6°
- Gold-plated T-clasp
- Steel crochet hook, U.S. size 6 (1.8mm)
- Scissors
- Multipurpose glue

Instructions

Pendant

Set aside 1 olive crystal drop and 2 orange/white beads. Randomly string rem beads onto thread.
Row 1: Leaving a 4"/10cm tail, ch 10; sl st into 1st ch to form a ring.
Next Row: *Ch 2, turn. Work 3 dc in each st; rep from * until you have a 10"/25cm chain. Work a bdc in next 3 sts. *Ch 2, turn. Work 3 dc in each st; rep from * until chain is 28"/71cm long, or desired length. Pull to secure, then cut thread, leaving a 4"/10cm tail.
Rows 3–4: Rep row 2 twice.
Row 5: *Ch 1, 1 bch; rep from* 9 times, sl st in sc of 1st ch, 1 sc in next 2 sts of row 4. Rep from * twice. Pull to secure, then cut thread, leaving a 4"/10cm tail.

Crocheted chain

String rem olive drop and orange/white beads onto thread.
Ch 4, sc in 2nd ch from hook, sc in next 2 ch sts.
Next Row: *Ch 2, turn. Work 3 dc in each st; rep from * until you have a 10"/25cm chain. Then work (3 bdc, 3 dc) in each st until chain is 28"/71cm long, or desired length. Pull to secure, then cut thread, leaving a 4"/10cm tail.

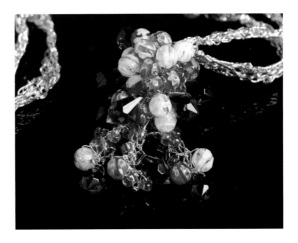

Finishing

Slide chain through top of pendant and position pendant at middle of chain. Secure pendant to chain by sc with beg tail Cut tails close to the work.

*Insert beg tail of crocheted chain into half of clasp. With crochet hook, pull tail through clasp twice, then sl st into any st of chain. Cut tail close to the work, then affix with a dot of glue. Rep as above with end tail and other half of clasp. Set aside until glue dries.

GLAMOUR NECKLACE

This elegant necklace features a rich variety of materials, including pearls, flower beads and crystals, all of which are harmoniously united by silver thread. The project is worked in several parts that are connected at the end. It is best worn with an elegant yet simple outfit since it completely steals the show. To make a set, it can be paired with the Evening at the Opera Bangle (pages 39–42).

Experience Level	◎ ◎ ◎ ◎ Experienced
Finished Measurements	Chain length: 20"/51cm; Pendant length: 10"/25cm
Special Techniques	Making crocheted bezels *(pages 21-22)*

Materials & Tools

- Silver metallic thread, approx 55yd/50m
- 1 silver flare oval flat-back Swarovski crystal, 30 x 22mm
- 3 flat-back pearl crystals, 12mm
- 4 silver-plated metal flowers, 5mm
- 1 silver with pearl tassel
- Silver-plated 2-strand box clasp
- 2 gold-plated jump rings, 4–5mm
- Multipurpose glue
- Black sewing thread
- Steel crochet hook, U.S. size 6 (1.8mm)
- Sewing needle
- Scissors
- Tapestry needle
- Pliers

Glamour Necklace and Evening at the Opera Bangle, pages 39–42.

Instructions

Special Stitches

Double crochet cluster (dc-cl): *Yo, insert hook in indicated st, and draw up a loop. Yo and draw through 2 loops on hook; rep from * once, yo and draw through all 3 loops on hook. *(page 17)*

Triple crochet cluster (tr-cl): *Yo twice, insert hook in indicated st and draw up a loop. (Yo and draw through 2 loops on hook) twice; rep from * once, yo and draw through all 3 loops on hook. *(page 17)*

Small 5-petal flower (make 7)

Leaving a 4"/10cm tail, ch 5; join with sl st into 1st ch to form a ring.

Rnd 1: *Ch 3, 2dc-cl in ring, ch 3, sl st into ring; rep from* 4 times (5 petals made). Pull to secure, then cut thread, leaving a 4"/10cm tail.

Large 5-petal flowers (make 2)

Leaving a 4"/10cm tail, ch 5; join with sl st into 1st ch to form a ring.

Rnd 1: *Ch 4, 2tr-cl in ring, ch 4, sl st into ring; rep from * 4 times (5 petals made). Pull to secure, then cut thread, leaving a 4"/10cm tail.

Crocheted circle

Leaving a 4"/10cm tail, ch 3; join with sl st into 1st ch to form a ring.

Rnd 1: Work 5 sc into center of ring; end with sl st into 2nd sc.

Rnd 2: Work 2 sc in each sc of 1st rnd; end with sl st into 1st sc—10 sc.

Rnd 3: Ch 2, *1 hdc in next st, ch 1; rep from * 9 times; end with sl st into 2nd ch st.

Rnd 4: Ch 2, 1 hdc in each st rnd; end with sl st in 1st ch—20 hdc.

Rnd 5: Ch 2, *1 hdc in next st, ch 1; rep from * 19 times; end with sl st into 1st ch.

Rnd 6: Rep rnd 5.

Rnd 7: Ch 2, 5 hdc in space of joining st of last rnd, sl st into next st, *ch 2, 5 hdc in next ch space, sl st into next st. Rep from *; end with sl st into 1st ch of rnd. Pull to secure, then cut thread, leaving a 4"/10cm tail.

Attaching oval crystal

Place oval crystal in center of crocheted circle. Thread sewing needle with black thread, but do not tie a knot at the end. Insert thread from WS to RS and make large sts all around crystal to mark its size. Remove crystal and set aside.

Rnd 1: With silver thread and crochet hook, pick up with surface crochet sts all around area marked with black thread; end with sl st into 1st st.

Rnd 2: Work sc all around; end with sl st into 1st sc. Pull thread to enlarge st on crochet hook. Remove hook but do not cut thread.

Spread glue evenly on WS of oval crystal and insert crystal into center of crocheted bezel. Carefully remove black thread. Set aside until glue dries. When dry, insert crochet hook into enlarged st and pull to fit crochet hook. Sl st all around. Pull to secure, then cut thread, leaving a 2"/5cm tail. With crochet hook, weave tail to WS.

Attaching small flowers

With tapestry needle and silver thread, sew 3 small flowers tog, side by side.
Cont to sew 2 big flowers under the small flowers. Cont to sew the circle under the large flowers. Place connected pieces on a flat surface, with RS facing. Place 2 small flowers on surface, with WS facing. Spread evenly with glue and attach each small flower to center of a large flower. Place 1 small flower on surface, with WS facing. Spread evenly with glue and attach on center of circle.

Crocheted chain

With crochet hook and silver thread, ch 3, sc into 2nd ch from hook, sc in next ch.
Ch 2 turn, *hdc in next 2 sts, ch 2, turn; rep from * until chain is 9"/23cm, or desired length.

Finishing

With sl st, attach 1 small flower to each end of crocheted chain. Cut ends and pull thread tightly to secure.

With crochet hook, weave beg tail into loops on one half of clasp, weaving tail through each loop, then through crocheted piece, until clasp is securely attached. Cut tail close to the work and apply a dot of glue to secure. Rep as above with end tail and other half of clasp.

Spread glue evenly on one side of each pearl and attach to centers of 2 small flowers. Spread glue evenly on one side of each metal flower and attach to rem 4 small flowers. With pliers, open jump ring and insert into center bottom of circle. Insert 1 small flower and attach tassel to bottom of flower. Spread glue on rem pearl and affix onto center of small flower. Set aside until glue dries.

GIANT FLOWER NECKLACE AND PENDANT

Make a statement with this eye-catching, multi-layered crocheted pendant. The flower is striking, with its bold size and sparkling Swarovski crystal set in the center. A sturdy brass ring is glued inside the flower, giving it enough weight to hang from the long crocheted necklace.

Experience Level	Experienced
Finished Measurements	Chain length: 22"/56cm; Pendant length: 4"/10cm
Materials & Tools	- Gold metallic thread, approx 33yd/30m - 1 brown oval flat-back Swarovski crystal, 18 x 13mm - 1 brass hoop, 2"/5cm diameter - Multipurpose glue - Steel crochet hook, U.S. size 6 (1.8mm) - Gold-plated T clasp - Scissors

Instructions

8-petal flower

Leaving a 4"/10cm tail, ch 2.

Rnd 1: Work 8 sc in 2nd ch from hook; join with sl st into 1st sc.

Rnd 2: Ch 1, 2 sc in each st in rnd; join with sl st into 1st sc—16 sc.

Rnd 3: Ch 1, 2 sc in 1st st, *sc in next st, work 2 sc in next st; rep from * around to last st. End with sc in last st; join with sl st into 1st sc—24 sc.

Rnd 4: Ch 1, sc in 1st st,*2 sc in next sc, sc in next 2 st; rep from * around to last 2 sts; end with 2 sc in next st, sc in last st; join with sl st into 1st sc—32 sc.

Rnd 5: Ch 4, 10 tr in same st, 10 tr in next st, 10 tr in next st, sc in next 2 sts; *ch 4, 10 tr in last sc of this rnd, 10 tr in next st, 10 tr in next st, sc in next 2 sts; rep from * 6 times making a total of 8 flower petals; end with sl st. Pull to secure, then cut thread, leaving a 4"/10cm tail.

Background circle

Rnds 1–4: Work same as for Flower 2.

Rnd 5: Ch 1, 2 sc in 1st st, *sc in next 3 st, 2 sc in next st; rep from * around to last 3 sts; end with sc in last 3 sts; join with sl st into 1st sc—40 sc.

5-petal flower

Leaving a 4"/10cm tail, ch 10; sl st into 1st ch to form a ring.

Rnd 1: Work 10 sc into ring; end with sl st into 1st sc.

Rnd 2: *Ch 3, tr in 1st sc 10 times, ch 3, sl st into same st (1st sc)—12 tr in all, (counting ch 3s as tr) sc in next sc; rep from * 4 times, to make a total of 5 flower petals; end with sl st. Pull to secure, then cut thread, leaving a 4"/10cm tail.

Rnd 6: Ch 1, work 2 sc in 1st st, sc in next 19 sts, 2 sc in next st, sc in last 19 sts; join with sl st into 1st sc—42 sc.

Rnd 7: Ch 1, 2 sc in 1st st, sc in next 20 sts, 2 sc in next st, sc in last 20 st; join with sl st into 1st sc—44 sc. Turn.

Rnd 8: *Ch 4, skip sc in next st; rep from * around; join with sl st into 1st sc of rnd 7—22 ch spaces.

Rnds 9–10: *Hdc in next ch space, sc in next sc; rep from * around 22 times in all; join with sl st into last st of rnd. Pull to secure, then cut thread, leaving a 4"/10cm tail.

Chain

Ch 3, work 2 sc in 2nd ch from hook, *ch 3, turn, dc in next 2 sts; rep from * until chain is 38"/97cm, or desired length. Pull to secure, then cut thread, leaving a 4"/10cm tail.

Finishing

Lay background circle on flat surface, with WS facing. Spread glue evenly on one side of brass hoop and press onto background circle, holding tog until affixed.

Spread glue evenly on other side of brass circle and on WS of 8-petal flower. Press flower onto brass circle, holding tog until affixed.

Spread glue evenly on WS of 5-petal flower and affix on center of 8-petal flower. Apply glue to back of crystal and press onto center of 5-petal flower. Set aside until glue dries.

Fold crocheted chain in half to mark the middle. Sc ending tail of background circle into marked middle of chain to attach pendant.

With crochet hook, weave beg tail of crocheted chain into loops on one half of clasp, weaving tail through each loop, then through crocheted piece, until clasp is securely attached. Cut tail close to the work and apply a dot of glue to secure. Rep as above with end tail and other half of clasp.

FIVE FINGERS NECKLACE

This striking necklace, made with gold thread and turquoise seed beads, is one of my favorites. When I can't decide whether I want to wear a short or long necklace, it's the perfect solution. The five chains in the piece, for me, represent the five people in my immediate family. Just as each family member is distinct but united to the others, so too are the chains in this necklace. To make a simple set, see the Turquoise Hoop Earrings (pages 92–94).

Experience Level	 Easy

Finished Measurements	Shortest chain length: 19"/48cm
	Longest chain length: 43"/109cm

Materials & Tools

- Gold metallic thread, approx 11yd/10m
- 532 turquoise seed beads, size 6°
- Gold-plated 5-strand box clasp
- Steel crochet hook, U.S. size 6 (1.8mm)
- Scissors
- Multipurpose glue

Instructions

Chain 1 (19"/48cm)

String 135 beads onto thread.

Ch 3, *1 bch with 3 beads tog, ch 1; rep from * 44 times, or until chain is 19"/48cm long; end with ch 3. Pull to secure, then cut thread, leaving a 4"/10cm tail.

Chain 2 (25"/64cm)

String 92 beads onto thread.

Ch 3, *1 bch with 2 beads, ch 2; rep from * 45 times, or until chain is 25"/64cm long; end with ch 3. Pull to secure, then cut thread, leaving a 4"/10cm tail.

Chain 3 (31"/78cm)

String 75 beads onto thread.

Ch 3, *1 bch, ch 1; rep from * 74 times, or until chain is 31"/78cm long; end with ch 3. Pull to secure, then cut thread, leaving a 4"/10cm tail.

Chain 4 (37"/94cm)

String 90 beads onto thread.

*Ch 15, 3 bch with 3 beads; rep from * 9 times, or until chain is 37"/94cm long. Pull to secure, then cut thread, leaving a 4"/10cm tail.

Chain 5 (43"/109cm)

String 140 beads on thread.

Ch 5, *10 bch, ch 5; rep from * 13 times, or until chain is 43"/109cm long. Pull to secure, then cut thread, leaving a 4"/10cm tail.

Finishing

With crochet hook, draw end tail of Chain 1 through 1st loop of one half of clasp. Pull gently, then sl st in 1st ch of finished chain. Rep once more, then sl st in 3 ch sts, and pull to secure. Cut thread tail close to the work and affix with a dot of glue. Weave end tail of same chain through 1st loop of other half of clasp, and rep from *.

Rep as above with Chains 2, 3, 4 and 5, making sure you secure each chain to corresponding loops on clasp halves. Set aside until glue dries.

DROP FOUNTAIN NECKLACE

This necklace combines natural amber stones with turquoise seed beads and gold dangling beads, creating a striking symphony of materials. The necklace is made of four separate crocheted chains that are knotted together in the middle with five turquoise quartz drops. It is perfectly suited to wear with a button-down shirt, tailored jacket or turtleneck.

Experience Level	◉ ◉ ◉ ◉ Easy
Finished Measurements	Length: 29"/74cm
Materials & Tools	- Gold metallic thread, approx 33yd/30m - 100 light amber chip beads, 5 x 10mm - 100 turquoise seed beads, size 6° - 12 gold-plated brass round filigree beads, 10mm - 5 turquoise quartz teardrops, 18 x 12mm to 24 x 14mm - Gold-plated 2-strand T clasp - Steel crochet hook, U.S. size 5 (1.9mm) - Multipurpose glue - Scissors

Drop Fountain Necklace and Gemstone Solitaire, pages 119–121.

Instructions

Chain 1 (18"/46cm)

Randomly string 25 beads onto thread. This assortment of beads should include 3 brass beads and several amber and turquoise seed beads. String 1 turquoise quartz drop bead, then randomly string 25 beads. Again, this assortment should include 3 brass beads and several amber and turquoise seed beads.
Ch 5, bch and ch randomly until you have worked 9"/23cm of chain using 30 beads.
You will now be at a turquoise drop. Bch with turquoise drop.
Cont to bch and ch randomly until you have worked 9"/23cm of chain, but this time using just 20 beads. 1 bch with 3 beads, 1 bch with 2 beads. sl st to 3rd ch from hook, sl st in next ch. Pull to secure, then cut thread, leaving a 4"/10cm tail.

Chain 2 (18"/46cm)

String beads as for Chain 1.
Ch 5, bch and ch randomly until you have worked 11"/28cm of chain using 30 beads. You will now be at a turquoise drop. Bch with turquoise drop.
Cont to bch and ch randomly until you have worked 7"/18cm of chain, this time using just 20 beads. 1 bch with 3 beads, 1 bch with 2 beads, sl st to 3rd ch from hook, sl st in next ch. Pull to secure, then cut thread, leaving a 4"/10cm tail.

Chains 3 and 4

Rep as for Chains 1 and 2.

Finishing

With crochet hook, weave beg tail of Chain 1 through one half of clasp, weaving tail through clasp then through crocheted piece, until securely attached. Cut tail close to the work and apply a dot of glue to secure.

Weave beg tail of Chain 2 through same half of clasp and rep as above. Rep as above with Chains 3 and 4, and other half of clasp.

Lay necklace on a flat surface so that sides are even. Wrap a piece of thread around all 4 chains, approx 12½"/32cm from clasp, and immediately below quartz drops. String rem quartz drop onto thread and tie a knot so that quartz drop hangs exactly in middle of necklace. Cut tail ends and affix with a bit of glue.

ELEMENTAL CHAIN

In this necklace, gold thread is crocheted onto a copper chain, giving the thread increased weight and creating a piece with a unique yet fashionable presence. As for the beads, I prefer brown—a trusty color that matches so many outfits. The necklace is surprisingly easy to make and is a great gift for any dear friend.

Experience Level	Easy
Finished Measurements	Length 44"/112cm

Materials & Tools

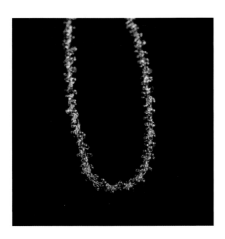

- Copper or brass unfinished chain, with 5mm round links, approx 31"/79cm
- Gold metallic thread, approx 11yd/10m
- Approx 150 bronze seed beads, size 6°
- Approx 50 fire-polished beads, various shades of brown, 4mm
- Gold-plated heart-shaped clasp
- Steel crochet hook, U.S. size 6 (1.8mm)
- Scissors
- Multipurpose glue

Instructions

Special Stitches

Crocheting into a metal chain *(page 21)*

Randomly string all beads onto thread and wrap beaded thread around bobbin.
Leaving a 4"/10cm, bsc into each link of chain until you reach the end of the chain, or desired length. Pull to secure, then cut thread, leaving a 4"/10cm tail.

Finishing

With crochet hook, weave beg tail into one half of clasp, weaving tail through loop and through crocheted piece until clasp is securely attached. Rep as above with end tail and other half of clasp. Cut tail close to the work and secure with a dot of glue.

GOLDEN DAISY NECKLACE

With gold thread and delicate pearls, this dramatic, elegant necklace is just right for a glamorous evening affair. The crochet pattern is made by changing the height of the stitches. The flowers and pearls add a delicate touch.

Experience Level	◉ ◉ ◉ ◉ Experienced
Finished Measurements	Length: 19"/48cm
Materials & Tools	- Gold metallic thread, approx 66yd/60m - Gold-plated 2-strand box clasp - 3 glass-based round pearl beads, 6mm - Steel crochet hook, U.S. size 6 (1.8mm) - Scissors - Multipurpose glue

Instructions

Crocheted chain

Foundation chain: Leaving a 4"/10cm tail, ch 113.

Row 1: Work 1 sc in 2nd ch from hook and in every ch until end of row, turn—112 sc.

Row 2: Ch 2, *skip 1 sc, 1 hdc, ch 1, rep from * to end of row, turn—112 sts.

Row 3: Ch 1, sc in next 31 sts, ch 2, hdc in next 10 sts, ch 1, dc in next 30 sts, hdc in next 10 sts, sc in next 31 sts; turn—112 sts.

Row 4: *Ch 3, skip 2, hdc in next 3 sts, ch 3, skip 2, sl st in next st; rep from * 13 more times, until end of chain; turn.

Row 5: Sl st in each of next 36 sts, *ch 6, skip 3, 6 dc in center of 3 hdc of prev row, ch 6, skip 2, sl st in next st; rep from * 4 times, sl st into next 36 sts until end of row. Pull to secure, then cut thread, leaving a 4"/10cm tail.

5-Petal Flowers (make 3)

Leaving a 4"/10cm tail, ch 4; join with sl st in 1st ch to form a ring.

Rnd 1 [RS]: Ch 1, sc into center of ring, *ch 4, sc in ring; rep from * 3 more times. Ch 4; join with sl st into 1st sc.

Rnd 2: Ch 1, (1 sc, 1 hdc, 2 dc, 1 hdc, 1 sc) into each ch-4 space; join with sl st into 1st sc. Turn to WS.

Rnd 3 [WS]: Ch 1, 1 sc in 1st sc of rnd 1,*ch 5, sc in next sc of 1st rnd; rep from * 4 more times. Ch 5; join with sl st into 1st sc of this rnd. Turn to RS.

Rnd 4 [RS]: Ch 1, (1 sc, 1 hdc, 3 dc, 1 hdc, 1 sc) in each ch-5 space of rnd 3; join with sl st into 1st sc. Pull to secure, then cut thread, leaving a 4"/10cm tail.

Weave tails through WS up to center of RS. String pearl bead onto tails and secure by weaving tails to WS. Tie tails tog in a knot on WS and cut ends.

Finishing

With crochet hook, weave beg tail of crocheted chain into loops of one half of clasp. Cut tail close to the work and affix with a dot with glue. Rep as above with end tail of chain and other half of clasp.

Apply glue evenly to WS of flowers. Affix 1 flower on center of necklace, and rem 2 flowers on either side of center flower. Set aside until glue dries.

COLLECTED TREASURES NECKLACE

It's hard to believe, but this elegant necklace is comprised of leftover beads from my bead box. The result is a long, exquisite piece made of five strands of crocheted bead chains. Like the Five Fingers Necklace (pages 77–79), this one also has five chains representing the five members of my family—each one beautiful individually and magnificent when connected.

Experience Level	 Easy
Finished Measurements	Length: 45"/114cm

Materials & Tools

- Gold metallic thread, approx 22yd/20m
- Approx 250 seed beads, various colors, size 6°
- Approx 250 fire-polished crystal beads, various colors, 4mm and 6mm
- Gold-plated 5-strand box clasp
- Steel crochet hook, U.S. size 6 (1.8mm)
- Scissors
- Multipurpose glue

Instructions

NOTE: ——————————————————————

When you notice that you have just a few beads left on the thread, string the remaining 250 beads onto the thread. I recommend working this way, since working with 500 beads on the thread can be difficult.

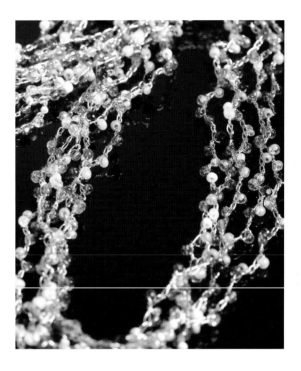

Randomly string 250 beads onto thread and wrap beaded thread around bobbin.

Chain (make 5)

Ch 3, *1 bch, ch 1; rep from * until chain is 37"/94cm long; end with ch 3. Pull to secure, then cut thread, leaving a 4"/10cm tail.

Finishing

With crochet hook, weave beg tail of chain into 1st loop of one half of clasp. *Wrap tail at least twice around loop, then sl st into chain, close to the loop. Pull tightly to secure. Cut tail close to the work and affix to chain with a dot of glue. Draw end tail of same chain into corresponding loop in other half of chain, and rep from *.
Rep as above with rem 4 chains, taking care to secure chain tails into corresponding loops in both clasp halves. Set aside until glue dries.

TURQUOISE HOOP EARRINGS

These unique earrings are based on a simple pair of store-bought hoops. The hoops are covered with gold-filled wire crocheted with tiny turquoise seed beads. The earrings can be worn on their own or matched up with the Five Fingers Necklace (pages 77–79).

Experience Level	◎ ◎ ◎ ◎ Easy
Finished Measurements	Diameter: 2"/5cm
Materials & Tools	- Dead-soft gold-filled wire, 28 gauge (0.3mm), approx 7yd/6.5m - Approx 200 turquoise seed beads, size 11° - 1 pair gold-filled round hoop earrings, 1¼"/3cm diameter - Steel crochet hook, U.S. size 5 (1.9mm) - Wire cutters - Pliers - Multipurpose glue

Five Fingers Necklace, pages 77–79, and Turquoise Hoop Earrings.

Instructions

Earring (make 2)

String approx 100 beads onto wire.
Leaving a 4"/10cm tail, *1 bsc with 3 beads
over hoop, 1 bch with 3 beads; rep from * until
hoop is completely covered. Cut wire, leaving a
20"/51cm tail.

With beg tail and starting at front of earring,
wrap crocheted chain around earring. Make sure
each wrap occurs between every 3-bch space,
and cont wrapping until earring is completely
wrapped.

NOTE:

*This wrap is what stabilizes and strengthens
the crocheted chain. Make sure the wrap is
strong, but take care not to rip the wire as
you wrap.*

Finishing

Wrap chain a few more times, then cut wire,
leaving 2"/5cm tails. Use pliers to closely
wrap tails around hoop, then apply a drop of
glue to affix.

DAZZLING BLUE ZIRCON EARRINGS

These truly dazzling yet lightweight earrings can be worn with ease day and night. Made with gold thread and blue zircon beads, they are perfectly matched with the Dazzling Blue Zircon Bangle (pages 46–48).

Experience Level	Intermediate
Finished Measurements	Length: 2"/5cm

Materials & Tools

- Gold metallic thread, approx 11yd/10m
- 184 blue zircon bicone Swarovski crystal beads, 4mm
- 1 pair gold-filled ear wires
- Steel crochet hook, U.S. size 6 (1.8mm)
- Scissors
- Multipurpose glue
- Tapestry needle

Instructions

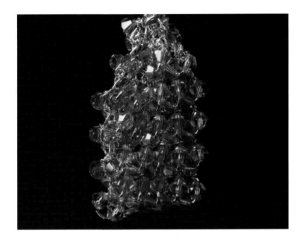

Row 11: 3 bsc with 2 beads in each st. Ch 1, turn.

Row 12: Sc in 3rd st from hook. Ch 1, turn.

Row 13: Sl st 1. Pull to secure, then cut thread, leaving a 4"/10cm tail.

Finishing

*With crochet hook, weave end tail through ear wire loop, insert hook into last st of earring, and gently pull thread to other side; rep from * one more time.

Sl st with beg tail close to ear wire loop and secure tightly. Cut tail close to the work and affix with a dot of glue.

NOTE:

There is no WS or RS in these earrings.

Earring (make 2)

String 92 beads onto thread.

Row 1: Leaving a 4"/10cm tail, ch 6.

Row 2: Bsc with 2 beads in 2nd ch from hook, 4 bsc with 2 beads in next 4 sts. Ch 1, turn.

Row 3: Work 5 bsc with 2 beads in each st, ch 1, turn.

Rows 4–9: Rep row 3.

Row 10: 1 bsc with 2 beads, skip next st, 1 bsc with 2 beads, skip next st, 1 bsc with 2 beads. (You have decreased this row to 3 bsc.) Ch 1, turn.

TWINKLING STAR EARRINGS

Playing with leftover materials is one of my favorite crocheting pastimes. All you need for these twinkling earrings is a handful of seed beads, a pair of ear posts and a bit of gold thread. The earrings take just minutes to make and are perfect for daily wear. To upgrade your look, wear them with the Five Fingers Necklace (pages 77–79) or the Collected Treasures Necklace (pages 89–91).

Experience Level	◉ ◉ ◉ ◉ Beginner
Finished Measurements	Diameter: 1"/2.5cm
Materials & Tools	- Gold metallic thread, approx 6yd/5.5m - 42 turquoise seed beads, size 6° - 1 pair gold-plated ear posts - Steel crochet hook, U.S. size 6 (1.8mm) - Scissors - Multipurpose glue

Twinkling Star Earrings and Collected Treasures Necklace, pages 89–91.

Instructions

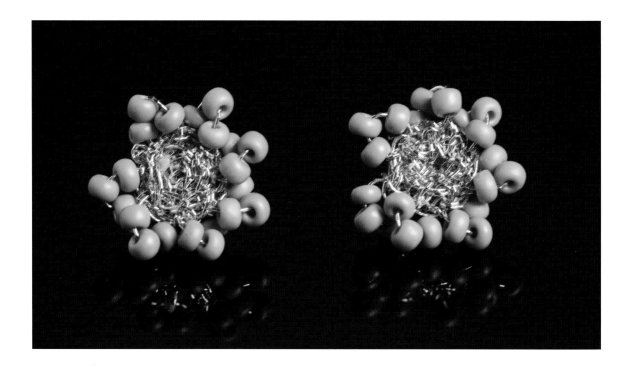

Earring (make 2)

String 21 beads onto thread.

Leaving a 4"/10cm tail, ch 3; join with sl st into 1st ch to form a ring.

Rnd 1: Work 3 sc into ring.

Rnd 2: Work 2 sc in next 3 sts all around (6 sc in all), sc in next st.

Rnd 3: Work 7 bsc with 3 beads; end with sl st in 1st bsc. Pull to secure, then cut thread, leaving a 4"/10cm tail.

Finishing

With crochet hook, weave tails to WS. Tie tails tog in a secure knot and cut close to the work. Apply a dot of glue to secure.

Spread glue evenly on ear post and WS of crocheted piece. Position crocheted piece on ear post. Hold tog to affix, then set aside until glue dries.

CREAM CLUSTER EARRINGS

I was delighted when I discovered that I could crochet with virtually anything, and I immediately tried using all kinds of materials. These earrings are made with white ribbon, pearls and seed beads. I save them for very special occasions and love matching them up with the Pearls on Ice Bracelet (pages 43–45).

Experience Level	Beginner
Finished Measurements	Diameter: 2"/5cm

Materials & Tools

- White ribbon, ⅜"/1cm wide, approx 11yd/10m
- Gold metallic thread, approx 11yd/10m
- 16 glass-based round pearl beads, 6 mm
- 20 white seed beads, size 6°
- 2 round crystal clear Swarovski crystals, 2mm
- 1 pair gold-plated ear wires
- Steel crochet hook, U.S. size E-4 (3.5mm)
- Scissors
- Multipurpose glue
- Pliers

Instructions

Rnd 2: Work 3 bsc in each st of rnd—18 bsc in all; end with sl st in 1st bsc to finish rnd. Pull to secure, then cut thread, leaving a 4"/10cm tail.

Finishing

With crochet hook, weave beg tail to WS and pull to secure. Weave end tail to RS, then to center WS of circle, and pull to secure. Tie tails tog in a secure knot, cut close to the work, and affix with a dot of glue. Make sure ends are invisible.

With pliers, open ear wire loop and slide into any st of last rnd of earring. Close loop securely. Apply a dot of glue to ear loop front and attach 1 round crystal. Set aside until glue dries.

NOTE:

This project is crocheted while holding ribbon and thread together.

Earring (make 2)

Randomly string 24 beads onto thread. Holding ribbon and thread tog, and leaving a 4"/10cm tail, ch 3; join with sl st in 1st ch to form a ring. Work 3 sc in center of ring; end with sl st in 1st sc.
Rnd 1: Work 2 bsc into each sc of ring—6 bsc in all; end with sl st in 1st bsc to finish rnd.

ROUNDED GOLDEN EARRINGS

These earrings are made with gold-filled wire and Japanese seed beads. They are part of my own collection of "essentials" since their neutral color makes them wearable anytime and anyplace. Light in weight, they can be worn all through the day and night. A real classic.

Experience Level	❁ ❁ ❁ ❁ Intermediate
Finished Measurements	Diameter: 1½"/4cm
Materials & Tools	- Dead-soft gold-filled wire, 28 gauge (0.3mm), approx 11yd/10m - 68 beige Japanese seed beads, size 8° - 1 pair gold-plated ear wires - Steel crochet hook, U.S. size 6 (1.8mm) - Wire cutters - Pliers

Instructions

Earring (make 2)

String 34 beads onto wire.
Leaving a 4"/10cm tail, ch 3; join with sl st
into 1st ch to form a ring.
Rnd 1: (Sc bsc, sc) into ring.
Rnd 2: *Sc in 1st st of ring, bsc in same st;
rep from * 2 more times—(3sc, 3 bsc); 6 sts
in all.
Rnd 3: *(1 sc 1, bsc) in same st; rep from
* 5 more times—12 sts.
Rnd 4: Bsc in each st around—12 bsc.
Rnd 5: Rep rnd 4. End with sl st. Pull to
secure, then cut wire, leaving a 2"/5cm tail.

Finishing

With crochet hook, weave tails from RS to
WS twice, then pull gently to secure. Cut tails
close to the work and push into the work. With
pliers, open ear wire loop and slide into any st
of last rnd of earring. Close loop securely.

WEB MANDALAS

These classic earrings are crocheted with gold-filled wire, creating a playful yet elegant look that reminds me of a mandala. Though the pattern is quite easy, working with wire takes a fair amount of skill and experience. Don't worry about making the circles perfectly round. In life, after all, not all circles are perfect.

Experience Level	Intermediate

Finished Measurements	Diameter: 2"/5cm

Materials & Tools

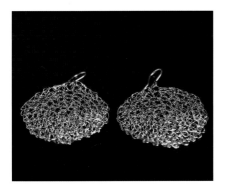

- Dead-soft gold-filled wire, 28 gauge (0.3mm), approx 16yd/15m
- 1 pair gold-plated ear wires
- Steel crochet hook, U.S. size 6 (1.8mm)
- Wire cutters
- Small hammer
- Pliers

Instructions

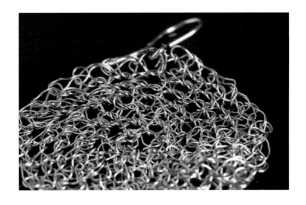

Finishing

With crochet hook, weave tails to WS, then cut wire close to the work. Lay work on a flat surface and tap gently with a small hammer to flatten.

With pliers, open ear wire loop and slide into any st of last round of earring. Close loop securely.

(Make 2)

Leaving a 4"/10cm tail, ch 4; join with sl st in 1st ch to form a ring.

Rnd 1: Ch 1, 10 sc in ring—10 sc.

Rnd 2: Ch 1, 2 sc in same st as joining and in each sc around; join with sl st into 1st sc—20 sc.

Rnd 3: Ch 1, 1 sc in same st as joining, 2 sc in next sc, *1 sc in next sc, 2 sc in next sc; rep from * around; join with sl st into 1st ch—30 sc.

Rnd 4: Ch 1, 1 sc in same st as joining and in next sc, 2 sc in next sc, *1 sc in each of next 2 sc, 2 sc in next sc; rep from * around; join with sl st into 1st sc—40 sc.

Rnd 5: Ch 1, 1 sc in same st as joining and in each of next 2 sc, 2 sc in next sc, *1 sc in each of next 3 sc, 2 sc in next sc; rep from * around; join with sl st into 1st ch—50 sts. Pull to secure, then cut wire, leaving a 4"/10cm tail.

CLUSTERED AMBER EARRINGS

Amber comes in many different shades, shapes and sizes, and I find it well-suited to crochet jewelry. It blends well with the style of the stitches and creates an organic look. Small amber beads are lightweight. This means they won't damage the thread and can be used to make earrings for all-day, comfortable wear.

Experience Level   ◉ ◉ ◉ ◉ Easy

Finished Measurements   Length: 3"/7.6cm

Materials & Tools
- Gold metallic thread, approx 11yd/10m
- Approx 14 amber dark bead chips, 5 x 11mm
- Approx 40 brown seed beads, size 6°
- Approx 40 gold seed beads, size 4°
- 2 gold-plated crimp ends, 4-5mm inside diameter
- 1 pair gold-plated ear wires
- Steel crochet hook, U.S. size 6 (1.8mm)
- Scissors
- Multipurpose glue
- Pliers

Instructions

Set aside 4 amber beads and randomly string rem beads onto thread.

Crocheted chain (make 4)

Leaving a 4"/10cm tail, ch 5, 10 bch with 2 beads tog, ch 5—20 sts. Pull to secure, then cut thread, leaving a 4"/10cm tail.

Finishing (rep twice)

Hold 2 crocheted chains tog and fold in half. Insert beg and end tails of chains into a crimp end. Add a dot of glue, then close crimp end with pliers. Cut tails close to crimp end. With pliers, open ear wire loop and slide into crimp end loop. Close loop securely. Apply a dot of glue to both crimp ends and ear wire front, and affix an amber bead on each. Set aside until glue dries.

GOLDEN DAISY EARRINGS

The lovely addition of metallic thread and pearls adds very little weight to these earrings, so you'll barely feel them even after a whole day's wear! Use ear posts for pierced ears, or clip-on posts if your ears are not pierced. They match perfectly with the Golden Daisy Bracelet (pages 27–29) and Golden Daisy Necklace (pages 86–88), and they also look great on their own.

Experience Level   Intermediate

Finished Measurements   Diameter: 1½"/4cm

Materials & Tools

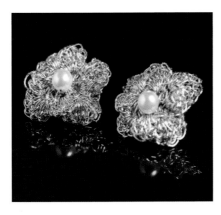

- Gold metallic thread, approx 11yd/10m
- 2 glass-based round pearl beads, 6mm
- 1 pair gold-plated ear posts and ear backs
- Steel crochet hook, U.S. size 6 (1.8mm)
- Scissors
- Multipurpose glue

Instructions

Finishing

Draw tails, from RS to WS, through hole in pearl bead. Tie a secure knot and cut tails close to the work. Apply a dot of glue to secure. Spread glue evenly on ear post and WS of crocheted piece. Position crocheted piece on ear post. Hold tog to affix, then set aside until glue dries.

Earring (make 2)

Leaving a 4"/10cm tail, ch 4; sl st into 1st ch to form a ring.

Rnd 1 [RS]: Ch 1, sc into center of ring; *ch 4, sc in ring; rep from * 3 more times (5 ch 4 sp). Ch 4; join with sl st into 1st sc.

Rnd 2: Ch 1, (1 sc, 1 hdc, 2 dc, 1 hdc, 1 sc) in each ch-4 space; join with sl st into 1st sc. Turn to WS.

Rnd 3 [WS]: Ch 1, sc in 1st sc of rnd 1,*ch 5 sc in next sc of 1st rnd; rep from * 4 more times. Ch 5; join with sl st into 1st sc of this rnd. Turn to RS.

Rnd 4 [RS]: Ch 1, (1 sc, 1 hdc, 3 dc, 1 hdc, 1 sc) in each ch-5 space of rnd 3; join with sl st into 1st sc. Pull to secure, then cut thread, leaving a 4"/10cm tail.

SUNBURST RING

This easy-to-make ring is an excellent way of using leftover beads from other projects. It's subtle enough to wear to the office but lovely enough to accompany evening wear.

Experience Level	⚙ ⚙ ⚙ ⚙ Beginner
Finished Measurements	Circumference: 2½"/6.4cm
Materials & Tools	- Gold metallic thread, approx 2yd/1.8m - 30 gold seed beads, size 6° - Gold-plated adjustable ring shank - Steel crochet hook, U.S. size 5 (1.9mm) - Scissors - Multipurpose glue

Gold and Silver Stretch Bracelet, pages 24–26, and Sunburst Ring.

Instructions

String all beads onto thread.

Leaving a 4"/10cm tail, ch 3; join with sl in 1st ch st to form a ring.

Work 5 sc into middle of ring.

Next Rnd: Work 2 sc in each sc—10 sc.

Next Rnd: Work bsc with 3 beads into every sc of prev rnd—10 bsc.

Next Rnd: sl st into each bsc—10 sl st.

With hook in last sc, and leaving a 4"/10cm tail, cut thread.

Finishing

Draw tail through last loop, remove crochet hook, and tighten. Insert hook in middle of circle and weave beg tail to WS of ring. Cut tails close to work.

Spread glue evenly on ring shank and WS of crocheted piece. Position crocheted piece on ring shank. Hold tog to affix, then set aside until glue dries.

GEMSTONE SOLITAIRE

I dearly love gemstones, but they are often too heavy to use for crochet jewelry. Since I just can't imagine making jewelry without the beauty of gemstones, I crocheted a setting for the amazonite bead in this ring. The bead fits snugly into the bezel and creates a lovely gemlike effect.

Experience Level	Experienced
Finished Measurements	Circumference: 2½"/6.4cm

Materials & Tools

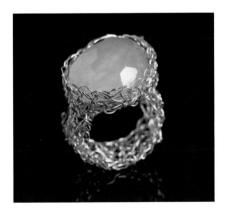

- Dead-soft gold-filled wire, 28 gauge (0.3mm), approx 6yd/5.5m
- 1 flat, round amazonite bead, 20 x 22mm
- Steel crochet hook, U.S. size 6 (1.8mm)
- Wire cutters
- Multipurpose glue

Gemstone Solitaire (front) and Drop Fountain Necklace, pages 80–82 (back).

Instructions

Leaving a 4"/10cm tail, ch 16; join with sl st into 1st ch st to form a ring.

Rnd 1: Sc into each ch of rnd.

Rnds 2–4: Sc into each sc.

Rnd 5: Work sc in each of next 5 sc, turn work 90° and work 3 sc across top of ring band, turn work 90°, work sc in next 5 sc, turn work 90°, work 3 sc across top of ring band to

Rnds 6–7: Sc in each of 16 sc of prev rnd.

Rnd 8: Sl st into each 16 sc of rnd 7. Pull to secure, then cut wire, leaving a 1½"/4cm tail.

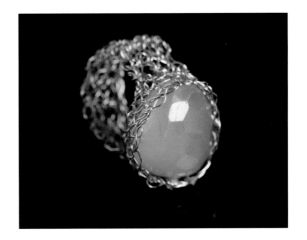

Finishing

With crochet hook, weave tails to WS of ring center and cut close to the work. Spread glue on back of bead, then push bead into ring center. Adjust until bead fits snugly into crocheted bezel, then set aside until glue dries.

Photo above, from left to right: Sunburst Ring, pages 116–118, Mixed Metals Medley Ring, pages 125–127, Teardrop Cluster Ring, pages 122–124.

TEARDROP CLUSTER RING

This delicate ring was the first piece of jewelry I sold overseas. After reviewing my entire collection of pieces, a buyer ordered 500 of these rings. I was delighted... but worried. How would I find the number of teardrop, glass-based pearl beads I needed? Luckily, a dear friend of mine drove to a crystal factory (in a snowstorm!) to pick up my special order.

Experience Level	◉ ◉ ◉ ◉ Intermediate
Finished Measurements	Circumference: 2½"/6.4cm
Materials & Tools	- Gold metallic thread, approx 6yd/5.5m - 18 glass-based teardrop pearl beads, 10 x 5mm - Gold-plated smooth ring shank - Steel crochet hook, U.S. size 6 (1.8mm) - Scissors - Multipurpose glue

Instructions

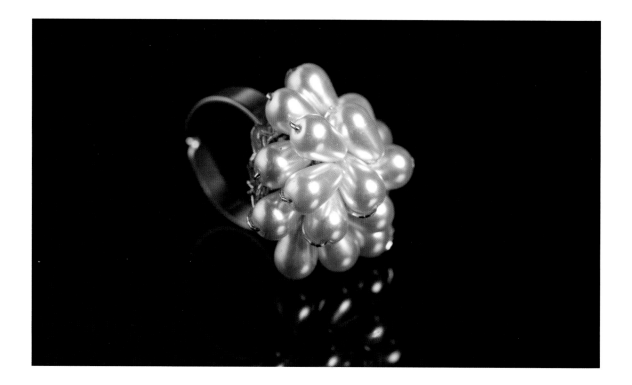

String all beads onto thread.

Leaving a 4"/10cm tail, ch 4; join with sl st into 1st ch to form a ring.

Rnd 1: *1 sc into ring, 1 bsc into ring; rep from * once—4 sts.

Rnd 2: *1 sc in next sc, 1 bsc in same sc; rep from * around—4 beads used.

Rep rnd 2 until all beads are used.

Next Rnd: Work 1 sc in each st of prev rnd; end with sl st. Pull to secure, then cut thread, leaving a 4"/10cm tail.

Finishing

With crochet hook, weave tails to WS and tie in a knot. Cut tails close to the work. Spread glue evenly on ring shank and WS of crocheted piece. Wrap crocheted piece around disc on top of ring. Hold tog to affix, then set aside until glue dries.

MIXED METALS MEDLEY RING

Crocheting with wire requires a lot of practice, and this project is just right for getting started. Gold-filled and silver wires are crocheted simultaneously, creating an unexpected combination of hues and adding stability to the ring. When determining the size of the ring, remember that it will expand a bit with wear. Also, be sure to work tightly.

Experience Level	Intermediate
Finished Measurements	Circumference: 2½"/6.4cm

Materials & Tools

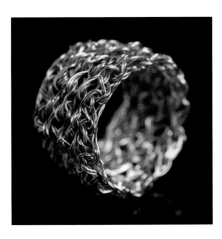

- Dead-soft gold-filled wire, 28 gauge (0.3mm), approx 6yd/5.5m
- Dead-soft silver wire, 28 gauge (0.3mm), approx 6yd/5.5m
- Steel crochet hook, U.S. size 1 (2mm)
- Wire cutters

Instructions

NOTE:

For this ring, work with both wires together.

Rnd 1: With both wires tog and leaving a 4"/10cm tail, ch 14, or desired length for ring size; join with sl st in 1st ch st to form a ring.

Rnd 2: Sc in every st of prev rnd.

Rnds 3–5: Rep 2nd row.

Rnd 6: Sl st in each sc around.

Pull to secure, then cut wires, leaving a 4"/10cm tail.

Finishing

With crochet hook, weave tails a few times into ring. Cut tails close to the work and push ends tightly into the work.

Index

Acknowledgments

To my mother, who put the crochet hook in my hand. She and my father have inspired and supported me every step in my life. Thank you!

To Rachel and Elan Penn, who turned my jewelry into a book. To Shoshana Brickman, who helped turn my work into words so pleasantly. To Orit Razily, the first believer, and the woman who gave the first hand and stage for my jewelry in Israel. To Aviva Ben-Sira, who gives an honorable stage for my jewelry at the Erez Israel Museum. To Gili Golan, who introduced my jewelry overseas, and who inspires me with her professional eye and wide knowledge of art and jewelry. To Lily and David Baron, my dear friends, who have helped my jewelry be exposed in Israel and overseas. To Sharon, my dear friend, who shows me the rainbow whenever it's raining. Thanks to Talia, who looks into my eyes and strengthens my soul. To Tammy, who saw my jewelry born, and believed. To Sigal, my friend from dancing days. Thank you for opening your heart whenever needed. To Anita, who threads my beads with love. A special thanks to every client who has bought my jewelry. Seeing you wear my handmade jewelry is what continues my passion to create.

And finally, to my private jewel box: Thanks to my three diamonds, Noam, Yael and Avigail, and to my dear husband, friend and partner, Arnon, the man who dances, sings and loves us all!